Everyday Maths

NEHA KHAITAN

RUPA

Published by
Rupa Publications India Pvt. Ltd 2021
7/16, Ansari Road, Daryaganj
New Delhi 110002

Sales centres:
Allahabad Bengaluru Chennai
Hyderabad Jaipur Kathmandu
Kolkata Mumbai

ISBN: 978-93-89967-34-0

First impression 2021

10 9 8 7 6 5 4 3 2 1

Excel Printers Pvt. Ltd, New Delhi

CONTENTS

AT THE TICKET COUNTER

TIMINGS

Trains to Mumbai:	8:30 a.m., 12 noon, 4:15 p.m.
Trains to Pune:	9 a.m., 1:20 p.m., 5:10 p.m.
Trains to Delhi:	10:15 a.m., 8 p.m.
Trains to Kolkata:	11 a.m., 11 p.m.

CHARGES

Mumbai First-Class:	₹250/
Mumbai Second-Class:	₹120/
Pune First-Class:	₹243/
Pune Second-Class:	₹126/
Delhi First-Class:	₹987/
Delhi Second-Class:	₹354/
Kolkata First-Class:	₹876/
Kolkata Second-Class:	₹359/

Look at the picture on Page 6 and answer the following questions.

(A)

1. How many people are there at the
   a. First ticket counter ☐
   b. Second ticket counter ☐
   c. Third ticket counter ☐

2. At Counter no. 3, the last two persons do not need tickets. They are in the queue to get some information. How many tickets does the ticket master at that counter sell? ☐

3. Two less than $\frac{1}{3}$ of the number of passengers need tickets to Delhi.
   a. How many need tickets to Delhi? ☐
   b. Among them, 3 need first-class tickets. How much do they spend together on first-class tickets? ☐
   c. The remaining passengers need second-class tickets. How much do they spend on second-class tickets? ☐

d. What is the difference of the amount spent on first-class and second-class tickets to Delhi? ☐

4. A person wants 2 first-class tickets and 1 second-class ticket to Kolkata. He pays the ticket cashier ₹2,500. How much does he get back? ☐

5. At Counter no. 2, 3 people need 2 first-class tickets each to Pune.

   a. How much do they spend together on tickets to Pune? ☐

   b. Of the remaining, 4 people need 1 second-class ticket each to Kolkata, and the rest need 1 second-class ticket each to Mumbai. What is the total amount spent by all the people at Counter no. 2? ☐

(B)

1. It is not noon yet. What is the time currently? (Hint: Time on the clock) ☐

2. Each person at Counter no. 1 takes 5 minutes at the counter.

a. What will be the time when the fourth member in the queue for Counter no. 1 gets her ticket? ☐

b. How long does the fifth person have to wait before he gets his turn at the counter? ☐

c. Will the eighth person be able to catch the first train to Kolkata? ☐

3. How long would it be before the next train to Delhi departs? ☐

4. What is the total number of trains plying between 8:15 a.m. and 4:40 p.m.? ☐

5. Each person at Counter no. 3 takes 2 minutes 30 seconds at the counter, while each person at Counter no. 2 takes 1 minute 15 seconds at the counter.

   a. The third person at Counter no. 2 says to the third person at Counter no. 3, 'I will wait for you till you are done.' How long does he wait? ☐

b. Who gets the ticket first? The last person in the queue for Counter no. 3 or the last person in the queue for Counter no. 2?

6. What is the time difference between:

   a. The first and the last train to Mumbai?

   b. The second and the third train to Pune?

   c. The first train to Delhi and the last train to Kolkata?

7. It takes 12 hours 35 minutes to reach Kolkata. A person takes the last train to Kolkata. When will he reach Kolkata?

8. A person walks into the station at the current time. He joins Counter no 3. Each person at the counter takes 2 minutes 30 seconds. What will be the time when he gets his ticket?

AT THE CAR PARK

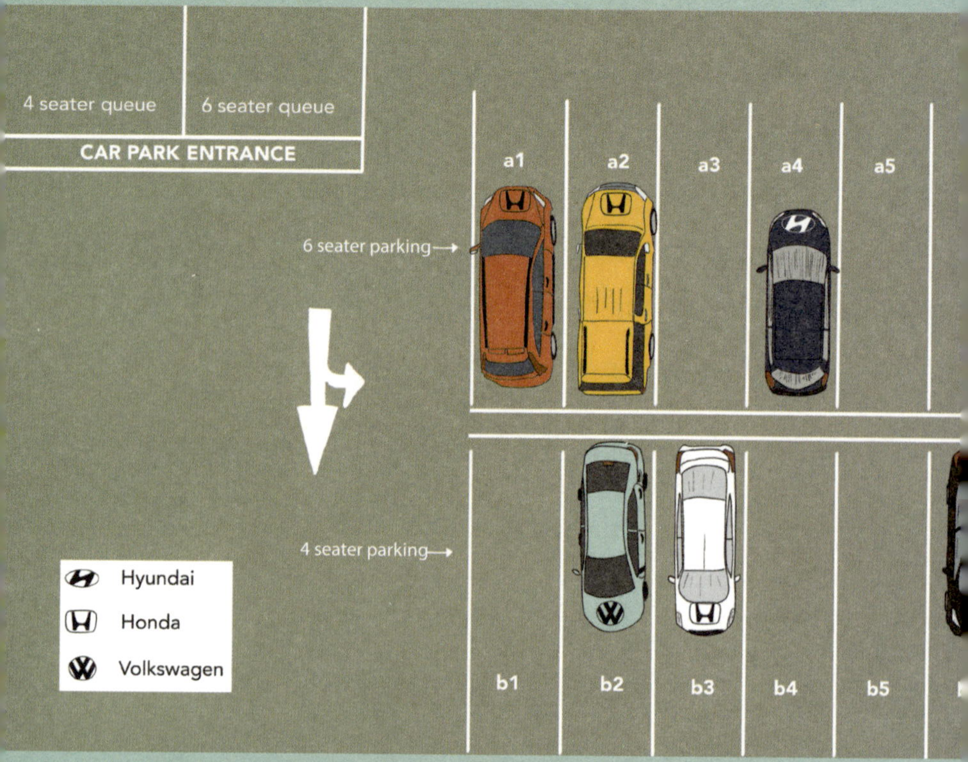
4 seater queue
6 seater queue
CAR PARK ENTRANCE
a1
a2
a3
a4
a5
6 seater parking
4 seater parking
Hyundai
Honda
Volkswagen
b1
b2
b3
b4
b5

Look at the picture on Page 12 and answer the following questions.

1. What fraction of the total cars is
   a. Hyundai
   b. Honda
   c. Volkswagen
   d. Honda and Volkswagen together

2. How many 6-seater Volkswagen cars are there?

3. What fraction of all 4-seater cars is Hyundai?

4. How many more 6-seater Hondas are there than 4-seater ones?

5. The cars in slots a2 and a4 leave and a 6-seater Hyundai and 4-seater Hyundai cars enter. If the cars cover minimum distance to occupy their slots,
   a. Which 6-seater slots get occupied?

b. Which 4-seaters slots get occupied? ☐

c. How many Hyundai cars are there? ☐

6. (Continued from Question 5.) A car waits at the queue if all the slots are full. 6 cars enter the parking lot in the following order: 4-seater, 4-seater, 6-seater, 6-seater, 4-seater, 6-seater.

   a. Are there any cars waiting? ☐

   b. If yes, in which queue and how many? ☐

   c. How many 6-seater slots are full? ☐

AT THE JUICE COUNTER

Dry Fruit Fudge
₹100/- per kg
Paper Glass
₹1.50 /-
Special Juice Recipe
100 ml Apple Juice +
100 ml Orange Juice +
50 ml Pomegranate Juice
Lime Juice (Large) ₹20/-
Lime Juice (Regular) ₹10/-
Banana Milk Shake (Large) ₹35/-
Banana Milk Shake (Regular) ₹20/-
Grape Juice (Large) ₹35/-
Grape Juice (Regular) ₹18/-
Fruit Salad ₹32/-
Apple Juice (per litre) ₹45/-
Orange Juice (per litre) ₹26/-
Pomegranate Juice (per litre) ₹54/-

Look at the picture on Page 16 and answer the following questions.

1. Rohit buys 2 large lime juice glasses. How much does he pay? ☐

2. Meena has ₹80.
   a. How many regular grape juice glasses can she buy? ☐
   b. What will be the amount left? ☐

3. The shopkeeper prepares Special Juice.
   a. What is the total quantity of the juice? ☐
   b. What is the cost? ☐

4. Read Question No. 3 again. If he makes 1 litre of Special Juice and divides it into 5 equal glasses,
   a. What is the cost of 1 litre of the juice? ☐
   b. How much juice is there in each glass? ☐

c. What is the cost of each glass (including that of the paper glass)? ☐

5. Read Question No. 4 again. He sells each glass of the drink at ₹2.50 more than the cost.

   a. How much is the selling price for each glass? ☐

   b. How much is the total profit? ☐

6. Shikhar buys 250 gm of the dry fruit fudge and 1 large lime juice for his train journey.

   a. What is the amount he pays for the fudge? ☐

   b. What is the total amount he pays? ☐

7. Neha buys 2 large banana milk shakes and 8 paper glasses and divides the juice equally into the glasses. If 1 large shake is 1 litre, then

   a. How much does she pay the shopkeeper? ☐

   b. How much does each glass hold? ☐

   c. What is the cost per glass of shake? ☐

8. Sunil wants to buy a plate of fruit salad, 750 gm of dry fruit fudge and 7 regular lime juice glasses.
   a. How much will this cost him? ☐
   b. He is short by ₹18.50. How much does he have? ☐

9. Priti buys 3 regular grape juice glasses and 3 litres of pomegranate juice. She gives the shopkeeper two 100-rupee notes and one 50-rupee note.
   a. How much does she give to the shopkeeper? ☐
   b. What is the total cost of the items? ☐
   c. How much should she get back? ☐
   d. She gets back two 10-rupee coins and six 2-rupee coins. How much more should she get back? ☐

INSIDE THE TRAIN

ONE SECTION OF A COACH

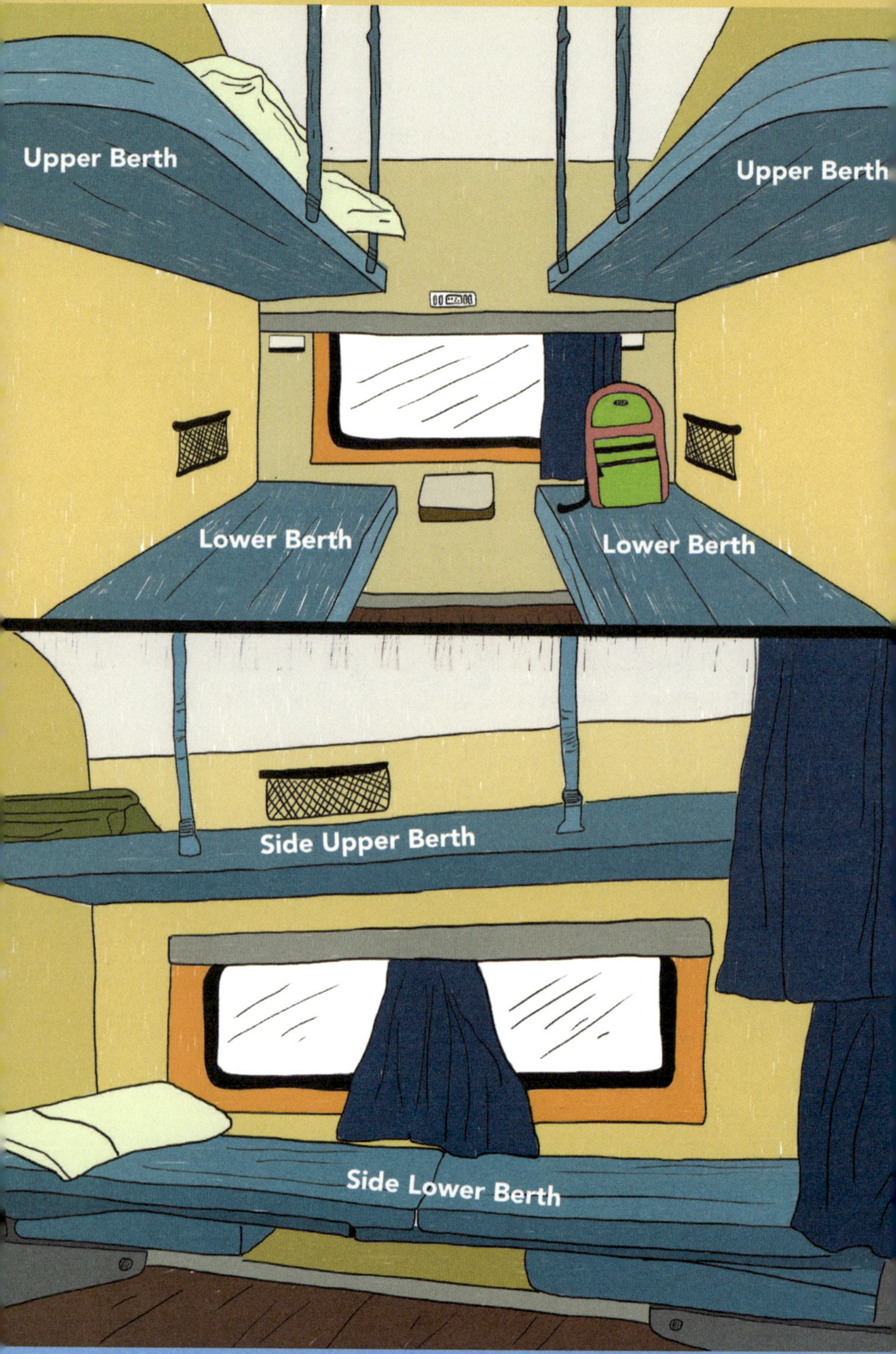

The picture on the facing page shows one section of a coach. The coach has seven such sections. Look at the image and answer the following questions.

1. How many
   a. Side Upper berths are there in all? ☐
   b. Side Lower berths are there in all? ☐
   c. Upper berths are there in all? ☐
   d. Lower berths are there in all? ☐

2. One person can sleep on each berth. How many people can fit into the coach? ☐

3. If a person has Wait List no. 5, how many people have to cancel for him to get a berth? ☐

4. 8 people cancel their tickets. And the number of wait-listed people boarding the train instead is 6.
   a. Will the train have any vacant berths? ☐
   b. If yes, how many? ☐
   c. There are 6 women in the coach who share their berths with their children. How many people does the coach contain? ☐

5. The coach is running full. The space below each lower berth and side lower berth can fit in 4 pieces of luggage.

$\frac{1}{3}$ of the all passengers has 3 pieces of luggage each.

$\frac{1}{7}$ of the remaining has 2 pieces of luggage each.

$\frac{1}{6}$ of the remaining has 5 pieces of luggage each.

$\frac{1}{6}$ of all the people have 1 piece of luggage each.

The remaining passengers have no luggage.

a. How many have 3 pieces of luggage each? ☐

b. How many have 2 pieces of luggage each? ☐

c. How many have more than 3 pieces of luggage each? ☐

d. How many have 1 piece of luggage each? ☐

e. How many have luggage? ☐

f. How many don't have any luggage? ☐

g. How many more pieces of luggage can be kept in the coach? ☐

AT THE RETIRING ROOM

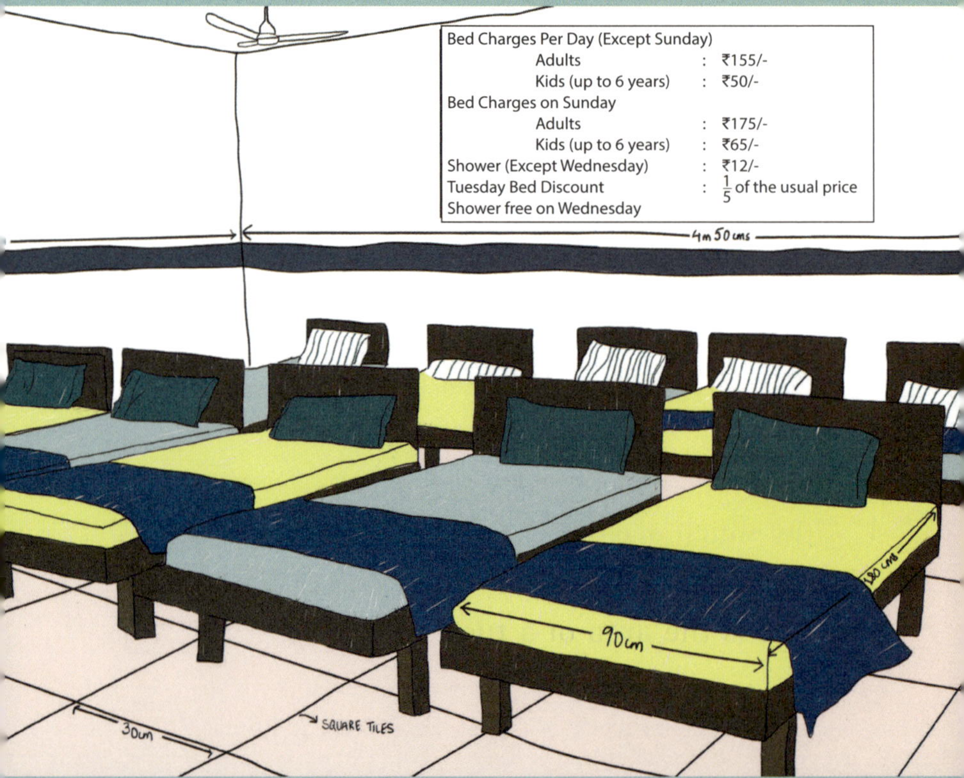

Bed Charges Per Day (Except Sunday)
Adults : ₹155/-
Kids (up to 6 years) : ₹50/-
Bed Charges on Sunday
Adults : ₹175/-
Kids (up to 6 years) : ₹65/-
Shower (Except Wednesday) : ₹12/-
Tuesday Bed Discount : $\frac{1}{5}$ of the usual price
Shower free on Wednesday
4m 50 cms
180 cms
90cm
30cm
SQUARE TILES

Look at the picture on Page 26 and answer the following questions.

(A)

(Unless specified, all people mentioned are adults)

1. What is the area of the room? ☐
2. What is the area of each bed? ☐
3. What is the total area of room occupied with beds? ☐
4. How much area of the room is free? ☐
5. What is the area of a tile? ☐
6. How many tiles are there in the room? ☐

(B)

1. Hari rents a bed every Monday, Wednesday and Friday. How much does he pay per week? ☐

2. Mohan rents a bed every Saturday and Sunday. How much does he pay for 2 weeks? ☐

3. Read the above two questions again. Deepa and Jaya rent a bed each on Monday. Sita, Meena and Reena rent a bed each on Monday and Tuesday

   a. How many beds are occupied on Monday? ☐

   b. How many beds are occupied on Tuesday? ☐

(C)

1. Sri uses the room on Wednesday and Thursday with shower. How much does he have to pay? ☐

2. Priya uses the room on Tuesday and Wednesday. She showers only on Tuesday. How much does she have to pay? ☐

(D)

1. Mahesh's family includes his wife and 2 kids aged 5 years and 10 years. He rents a bed for each family member for a Sunday (including himself). Only his children use the shower.
   a. How much does he pay in all? ☐
   b. How much does he pay for shower alone? ☐
   c. How many beds will be unoccupied that day, if there are no other people in the room? ☐

2. (Continued from the previous question) On the same day, Mahesh uses the room, Ram, his two brothers, and four friends miss their train. And they together want a place to rest. Will all of them be able to rent a bed? ☐

AT THE CLOAK ROOM

CLOAK ROOM CHARGES

0–12 hrs	:	₹25 per bag/suitcase
13–24 hrs	:	₹48 per bag/suitcase
25–48 hrs	:	₹60.50 per bag/suitcase
>48 hrs	:	₹115.75 per bag/suitcase

Look at the picture on Page 32 and answer the following questions.

(A)

1. Complete the table.

Name	Total Pieces of Luggage	Total Weight of Luggage (kg)
Ram		
Sam		
Mina		
Dilip		
Rita		
Roy		

2. What is the total weight of the entire luggage?

3. How much more weight can Shelf 1 take?

4. I want to add a 30-kg bag to Shelf 2. Will it be within the weight limit? ☐

5. Sam wants to replace his bag with a 22-kg bag in Shelf 2. Will it be within the weight limit? ☐

6. I add a 27-kg suitcase and a 9-kg bag to Shelf 3. What is the total weight on Shelf 3 after those are added? ☐

7. I want to add a 27-cm suitcase to the left of Mina's bag in Shelf 2. Will it fit? ☐

8. If Ram removes all his bags,
   a. What will be the total weight of the entire luggage? ☐
   b. How much more weight will Shelf 3 take? ☐
   c. How much space will remain in Shelf 1? ☐

(B)

1. Rita leaves her luggage for 28 hours. How much does she have to pay? ☐

2. Sam left his luggage from 10 a.m. to 6 p.m.
   a. For how long did he leave his luggage in the cloakroom? ☐
   b. How much does he have to pay? ☐

3. Ram leaves 1 piece of luggage for 20 hours and the remaining for 50 hours.
   a. How many bags does he leave for 50 hours? ☐
   b. How much does he pay in all? ☐

4. What is the difference in weight of the luggage of Sam and Mina? ☐

5. Mina leaves her luggage for a day. How much does she pay? ☐

6. Of all the pieces of luggage present in the room,
   a. What is the weight of the heaviest piece of luggage? ☐
   b. What is the weight of the lightest piece of luggage? ☐
   c. How much heavier is the heaviest piece than the lightest piece? ☐

NOTES FOR TEACHERS

AT THE CAR PARK

1. Teachers might talk about the two different entrances for the 6-seater and 4-seater queues.

2. When the car slots get full, the cars wait at the respective queues. And the first one that reaches the queue leaves first to occupy the slots as they get empty.

3. Question no. 5. The minimum distance means the first available slot. There might be other slots available too, but the car only occupies the first available one in the row.

AT THE JUICE COUNTER

1. Question no. 3. Here, we are talking about the cost of making the special juice (looking at the recipe in the picture) with reference to the prices mentioned in the price chart.

2. Question no 4. This follows from Question no. 3, where we are adding a profit to the cost calculated above.

INSIDE THE TRAIN

1. Upper berth means the normal upper berth (not including the side upper berths). Same for lower berths.

2. Teachers might need to explain the concept of wait list to the students. They can draw a train coach block diagram showing all seats being full and a separate list on which names get wait listed when the train coach is full.

AT THE RETIRING ROOM

1. Teachers might need to explain to the students that the unseen part of the wall includes the length of the room.

2. Part B: The answers of 3a and 3b depend on the outcome of questions 1 and 2.

AT THE CLOAK ROOM

1. Teachers might need to explain to the students that the unseen part of the shelves includes the entire length.

Rough Work

ANSWERS

AT THE TICKET COUNTER (A)

1a - 10

1b - 10

1c - 10

2 - 8

3a - 8

3b - ₹2,961

3c - ₹1,770

3d - ₹1,191

4 - ₹389

5a - ₹1,458

5b - ₹3,254

AT THE TICKET COUNTER (B)

1 - 10:30 a.m.

2a - 10:50 a.m.

2b - 20 minutes

2c – No (It takes 40 minutes, so she gets her ticket at 11:10 a.m.)

3 – 9 hours 30 minutes (next train to Delhi is at 8 p.m.)

4 – 7

5a – 3 minutes 45 seconds

5b – The last person in the queue for Counter no. 2

6a – 7 hours 45 minutes

6b – 3 hours 50 minutes

6c – 12 hours 45 minutes

7 – 11:35 a.m. on the following day

8 – 10:57:30 a.m.

AT THE CAR PARK

1a – $\frac{1}{6}$

1b – $\frac{1}{2}$

1c – $\frac{1}{3}$

1d – $\frac{5}{6}$

2 – None

3 – 0

4 – 1

5a – a1 Honda, a2 Hyundai, _, _, _,

5b – b1 Hyundai, b2 Volkswagen, b3 Honda, _, _,

b6 Volkswagen

5c – 2

6a – Yes

6b – 4-seater queue – 1

6c – 5

AT THE JUICE COUNTER

1 – ₹40

2a – 4

2b – ₹8

3a – 250 ml

3b – ₹9.80

4a – ₹39.20

4b – 200 ml

4c – ₹9.34

5a – ₹11.84

5b – ₹12.50

6a – ₹25

6b – ₹45

7a – ₹82

7b – 250 ml

7c – ₹10.25

8a – ₹177

8b – ₹158.50

9a – ₹250

9b – ₹216

9c – ₹34

9d – ₹2

INSIDE THE TRAIN

1a – 7

1b – 7

1c – 14

1d – 14

2 – 42

3 – 5

4a – Yes

4b – 2

4c – 46

5a – 14

5b – 4

5c – 4

5d – 7

5e – 29

5f – 13

5g – 7

AT THE RETIRING ROOM (A)

1 – 27 sq. m

2 – 1.62 sq. m

3 – 16.2 sq. m

4 – 10.8 sq. m

5 – 900 sq. cm

6 – 300 tiles

AT THE RETIRING ROOM (B)

1 – ₹465

2 – ₹660

3a – 6 (including Hari)

3b – 3

AT THE RETIRING ROOM (C)

1 – ₹322

2 – ₹291

AT THE RETIRING ROOM (D)

1a – ₹614

1b – ₹24

1c – 6

2 – No, they are 7 in all and there is space for 6

AT THE CLOAK ROOM (A)

1

Name	Total Number of Luggage	Total Weight of Luggage (in kgs)
Ram	3	75.5
Sam	3	60.5
Mina	2	42.5
Dilip	1	24
Rita	2	41
Roy	1	25.4

2 – 268.9

3 – 70 kgs

4 – Yes (It can take 67.6 kgs more)

5 – Yes

6 – 127.5 kgs

7 – No. (The space available is 21 cms)

8a – 193 kgs 400 gms

8b – 257 kgs

8c – 83 cms

AT THE CLOAK ROOM (B)

1 – ₹121

2a – 8 hours

2b – ₹75

3a – 2 bags

3b – ₹279.5

4 – 18 kgs

5 – ₹96

6a – Ram's (28.5 kgs)

6b – Sam's (16 kgs)

6c – 12.5 kgs